C000108142

contents

British & North American Readers
Please note that Australian cup and spoon
measurements are metric. A quick conversion
guide appears on page 63.

chicken and sweet soy stir-fry

You need to purchase a large barbecue chicken,
weighing approximately 900g, for this recipe.

450g hokkien noodles
1 tablespoon peanut oil
3 cups (510g) coarsely chopped cooked chicken
6 green onions, sliced
1 teaspoon bottled crushed garlic
2 cups (160g) bean sprouts
$1/2$ cup (125ml) chicken stock
2 tablespoons sweet chilli sauce
$1/4$ cup (60ml) kecap manis

Place noodles in small heatproof bowl; cover
with boiling water, separate with fork, drain.
Heat oil in wok or large frying pan; cook chicken,
onion and garlic until chicken is heated through.
Add noodles, sprouts and combined stock,
sauce and kecap manis; stir-fry until noodles
are heated through.

serves 4
per serving 14.5g fat; 1668kJ (398 cal)

fresh tomato and chilli pasta

500g penne
1/3 cup (80ml) olive oil
2 teaspoons bottled crushed garlic
2 teaspoons bottled chopped chilli
4 medium ripe tomatoes (800g), chopped
1 cup chopped fresh flat-leaf parsley
1/2 cup (40g) parmesan flakes

Cook pasta in large saucepan of boiling water, uncovered, until just tender; drain.
Meanwhile, heat oil in large frying pan, add garlic and chilli; cook, stirring, about 1 minute or until fragrant. Add tomato and parsley; remove from heat.
Add sauce mixture to pasta; toss gently. Serve topped with cheese.

serves 4
per serving 19.9g fat; 2547kJ (608 cal)

burghul and fetta salad

1^1/$_2$ cups (240g) burghul
200g green beans
^{1}/$_3$ cup (80ml) oil-free french dressing
2 tablespoons lemon juice
1^1/$_2$ cups firmly packed fresh flat-leaf parsley
^{1}/$_2$ cup chopped fresh mint
4 green onions, sliced
250g cherry tomatoes, halved
200g fetta cheese, crumbled

Place burghul in large bowl; cover with boiling water, set aside about 10 minutes or until burghul is just tender, drain. Using absorbent paper, pat burghul dry.
Meanwhile, cut beans into thirds. Boil, steam or microwave until just tender; drain.
Combine burghul, beans, dressing, juice and remaining ingredients in large bowl; toss gently.

serves 4
per serving 13g fat; 1522kJ (364 cal)

chilli prawn linguine

500g linguine
$^1/_3$ cup (80ml) olive oil
400g small peeled prawns
3 small fresh red chillies, sliced finely
1 teaspoon bottled crushed garlic
$^1/_2$ cup chopped fresh flat-leaf parsley
2 teaspoons grated lemon rind

Cook pasta in large saucepan of boiling water,
uncovered, until just tender; drain.
Meanwhile, heat oil in large frying pan,
add prawns, chilli and garlic; cook, stirring,
until prawns are just cooked through.
Remove from heat, stir in parsley and lemon rind.
Combine pasta with prawn mixture and
toss gently before serving.

serves 4
per serving 20.5g fat; 2712kJ (648 cal)

pasta with creamy bacon sauce

500g penne
1 tablespoon olive oil
1 large leek (500g), sliced
4 rashers bacon (280g), chopped coarsely
1 teaspoon bottled crushed garlic
2 large zucchini (300g), sliced
350g button mushrooms, halved
2 tablespoons dijon mustard
1¼ cups (300g) light sour cream
¾ cup (180ml) milk

Cook pasta in large saucepan of boiling water,
uncovered, until just tender; drain.
Meanwhile, heat oil in large frying pan,
add leek, bacon and garlic; cook, stirring,
until leek is soft and bacon is browned.
Add zucchini and mushrooms to pan;
cook, stirring, until zucchini is just tender.
Stir in mustard, sour cream and milk;
cook, stirring, until hot.
Toss sauce through pasta before serving.

serves 4
per serving 28g fat; 3252kJ (777 cal)

tandoori lamb with
tomato sambal and mint raita

12 lamb cutlets (900g)
1/4 cup (75g) tandoori paste
3/4 cup (200g) yogurt
2 medium tomatoes (380g)
1 lebanese cucumber (130g)
1 small red onion (100g)
1 tablespoon lemon juice
1 teaspoon bottled crushed garlic
2 tablespoons fresh mint
2 tablespoons fresh coriander
4 naan bread

Combine lamb with paste and 1/4 cup (70g) of the yogurt in large bowl; mix well.
Cook lamb in batches on heated oiled grill plate (or grill or barbecue) until browned on both sides and cooked as desired.
Meanwhile, chop tomatoes, cucumber and onion; combine in medium bowl with juice and garlic.
Blend or process remaining yogurt with mint and coriander until smooth (yogurt will become runny).
Grill naan until warm. Serve cutlets with tomato sambal, mint raita and naan.

serves 4
per serving 24.4g fat; 2312kJ (552 cal)

fish with wasabi mayonnaise

1 tablespoon peanut oil
4 firm white fish fillets (800g)
1/3 cup (100g) mayonnaise
1-2 tablespoons wasabi paste, to taste
2 green onions, chopped finely
2 tablespoons chopped fresh coriander
2 tablespoons lime juice

Heat oil in large non-stick frying pan, add fish;
cook until browned on both sides and just
cooked through.
Meanwhile, combine mayonnaise, wasabi,
onion, coriander and juice in small bowl.
Serve fish with wasabi mayonnaise and,
if desired, steamed chinese broccoli.

serves 4
per serving 17.6g fat; 1454kJ (347 cal)

pork butterfly steaks with radicchio

4 pork butterfly steaks (625g)
1 teaspoon fennel seeds, crushed
2 tablespoons olive oil
1 large radicchio (500g)
3 bacon rashers (210g), chopped
1 teaspoon bottled crushed garlic
4 small egg tomatoes (240g), sliced thickly
1 tablespoon red wine vinegar
1 teaspoon brown sugar

Sprinkle both sides of pork steaks with fennel seeds.
Heat half of the oil in large frying pan; cook pork until browned on both sides and just cooked through. Remove from pan; cover to keep warm.
Meanwhile, cut radicchio into quarters, remove core, then cut each wedge in half.
Add bacon to same pan; cook, stirring, until browned and crisp. Add remaining olive oil, garlic, radicchio, tomato, vinegar and sugar to pan; cook, stirring, until lettuce is just wilted.
Serve pork with hot radicchio mixture.

serves 4
per serving 18.5g fat; 1482kJ (354 cal)

pork and chinese broccoli stir-fry

500g fresh singapore noodles
2 tablespoons peanut oil
750g pork strips
1 large brown onion (200g), sliced
1 teaspoon bottled crushed garlic
1kg chinese broccoli, chopped coarsely
$1/3$ cup (80ml) oyster sauce
1 tablespoon soy sauce

Place noodles in large heatproof bowl,
cover with boiling water, stir gently to
separate noodles; drain.
Heat half of the oil in wok or large frying pan;
stir-fry pork, in batches, until browned and
cooked through.
Heat remaining oil in same wok; stir-fry onion
and garlic until onion is soft. Return pork to wok
with broccoli, combined sauces and noodles;
stir-fry until broccoli is just wilted.

serves 4
per serving 24.4g fat; 2347kJ (561 cal)

lamb and mango salad with sweet chilli dressing

600g lamb fillets
1 tablespoon sesame oil
1 medium red onion (150g), sliced thinly
2 medium mangoes (860g), sliced
250g cherry tomatoes, halved
1 cup (80g) bean sprouts
1 cup chopped fresh coriander
$^1/_4$ cup (60ml) sweet chilli sauce
1 tablespoon rice wine vinegar

Brush lamb with oil and cook on heated oiled grill plate (or grill or barbecue) until browned all over and cooked as desired.
Combine onion, mango, tomato, sprouts and coriander in large bowl.
Thinly slice lamb and toss through salad with combined sauce and vinegar.

serves 4
per serving 10.9g fat; 1433kJ (342 cal)

chicken laksa

You need to purchase a large barbecue chicken,
weighing approximately 900g, for this recipe.

450g fresh egg noodles
1 teaspoon peanut oil
$1/4$ cup (75g) laksa paste
$3^1/4$ cups (810ml) light coconut milk
1 litre (4 cups) chicken stock
2 tablespoons lime juice
1 tablespoon sugar
1 tablespoon fish sauce
6 kaffir lime leaves, torn
3 cups (510g) coarsely chopped cooked chicken
1 cup (80g) bean sprouts
$1/2$ cup loosely packed fresh mint leaves

Rinse noodles in strainer under hot running water.
Separate noodles with fork; drain.
Heat oil in large saucepan; cook paste, stirring,
until fragrant. Stir in coconut milk, stock, juice,
sugar, sauce and lime leaves; bring to a boil.
Reduce heat; simmer, covered, 3 minutes.
Add chicken; stir until laksa is heated through.
Divide noodles among serving bowls. Ladle laksa
over noodles; top with sprouts and mint.

serves 4
per serving 24.4g fat; 2351kJ (561 cal)

sausages with lentil and vegetable sauce

8 beef sausages
1 tablespoon olive oil
1 medium brown onion (150g), chopped finely
1 teaspoon bottled crushed garlic
2 trimmed celery sticks (150g), chopped finely
3 bacon rashers (210g), chopped
2 medium zucchini (240g), sliced
1/2 cup (125ml) chicken stock
400g can tomatoes
1 teaspoon bottled chopped chilli
1 tablespoon tomato paste
410g can brown lentils, rinsed, drained
2 teaspoons chopped fresh thyme

Cook sausages on heated grill plate
(or grill or barbecue) until browned all over
and cooked through.
Meanwhile, heat oil in medium saucepan,
add onion and garlic; cook, stirring, until onion
softens. Add celery, bacon and zucchini;
cook, stirring, until celery softens.
Stir in stock, undrained crushed tomatoes,
chilli and paste; bring to a boil. Add lentils; stir
until heated through. Serve lentil and vegetable
sauce with sausages, sprinkled with thyme.

serves 4
per serving 48g fat; 2625kJ (628 cal)

swordfish with thai dressing

4 swordfish steaks (800g)
1/3 cup (80ml) sweet chilli sauce
1/2 cup (125ml) lime juice
1 tablespoon fish sauce
2 teaspoons finely chopped fresh lemon grass
2 tablespoons finely chopped fresh coriander
1/2 cup finely chopped fresh mint
1 teaspoon grated fresh ginger

Cook fish on heated oiled grill plate (or grill or barbecue) until browned both sides and cooked as desired.
Combine remaining ingredients in screw-top jar; shake well. Drizzle dressing over fish.
Serve with lemon wedges and a salad of mixed leaves, if desired.

serves 4
per serving 5.1g fat; 1006kJ (241 cal)

steak and aïoli sandwiches

8 thin beef fillet steaks (800g)
4 large egg tomatoes (360g), halved
1 tablespoon olive oil
1/2 cup (75g) mayonnaise
1 teaspoon bottled crushed garlic
4 slices ciabatta
1 tablespoon shredded fresh basil
1 tablespoon balsamic vinegar
100g mesclun

Cook beef on heated oiled grill plate (or grill
or barbecue) until browned on both sides and
cooked as desired.
Meanwhile, place tomatoes, cut-side up,
on grill tray; drizzle with oil. Grill 10 minutes
or until softened.
Combine mayonnaise and garlic in small bowl.
Toast bread, spread with mayonnaise mixture
(aïoli); top with steaks and tomatoes, sprinkle with
basil and vinegar. Serve with mesclun.

serves 4
per serving 20.9g fat; 1795kJ (429 cal)

grilled lamb cutlets with butter bean and tomato salad

12 lamb cutlets (900g)
1 tablespoon celery salt
2 x 300g cans butter beans, rinsed, drained
3 trimmed celery sticks (225g), chopped coarsely
1 medium red onion (170g), chopped finely
4 medium tomatoes (760g), chopped
$1/3$ cup chopped fresh flat-leaf parsley
2 tablespoons lemon juice
1 teaspoon bottled crushed garlic

Sprinkle lamb on both sides with celery salt.
Cook lamb on heated oiled grill plate (or grill
or barbecue) until lamb is browned on both sides
and cooked as desired.
Meanwhile, combine remaining ingredients in
large bowl. Serve lamb cutlets with bean salad.

serves 4
per serving 10.8g fat; 1068kJ (255 cal)

red curry pork with basil

1 medium red capsicum (200g)
1 medium green capsicum (200g)
1 medium yellow capsicum (200g)
8 thin pork steaks (650g)
2 tablespoons thai red curry paste
140ml can coconut cream
1 tablespoon peanut oil
³/₄ cup (180ml) chicken stock
¹/₄ cup shredded fresh basil

Quarter capsicums, remove seeds and
membranes. Cook on heated oiled grill plate
(or grill or barbecue) until just tender.
Spread each pork steak with ¹/₂ teaspoon
curry paste and 2 teaspoons coconut cream.
Fold in half to seal.
Heat oil in large non-stick frying pan. Add pork;
cook until browned on both sides and cooked
through. Remove from pan; cover to keep warm.
Add remaining paste to same pan; cook, stirring,
until fragrant. Add stock; bring to a boil. Stir in
remaining coconut cream and basil until heated
through. Serve pork with sauce, capsicum and,
if desired, steamed rice.

serves 4
per serving 20.1g fat; 1538kJ (368 cal)

pork with white wine sauce

1 tablespoon olive oil
4 x 180g pork scotch fillet steaks
$1/2$ cup (125ml) dry white wine
$1/2$ cup (125ml) chicken stock
50g butter, chopped
2 tablespoons chopped fresh flat-leaf parsley

Heat oil in large frying pan; cook pork,
in batches, until browned on both sides and
just cooked through. Cover to keep warm.
Add wine to same pan, bring to a boil; add stock
and simmer, uncovered, until reduced by a third.
Stir in butter until melted; stir in parsley.
Cut pork into slices; serve with white wine
sauce and, if desired, steamed baby potatoes
and sugar snap peas.

serves 4
per serving 21.2g fat; 1561kJ (373 cal)

veal stroganoff with buttered sage pasta

250g ricciolini pasta (or other short pasta)
1 tablespoon olive oil
1 small brown onion (80g), sliced thinly
1 teaspoon bottled crushed garlic
2 teaspoons sweet paprika
600g veal steaks, sliced thinly
100g cup mushrooms, sliced thickly
100g button mushrooms, sliced thickly
1/4 cup (60ml) red wine
1 tablespoon tomato paste
1/2 cup (120g) sour cream
1/2 cup (125ml) beef stock
2 teaspoons cornflour
1 tablespoon chopped fresh sage
30g butter
50g baby spinach leaves

Cook pasta in large saucepan of boiling water, uncovered, until just tender.
Meanwhile, heat oil in medium saucepan, add onion, garlic and paprika; cook, stirring, until onion softens. Add veal; cook, stirring, until veal is browned all over.
Add mushrooms to pan; cook, stirring, until mushrooms are tender. Add wine; bring to a boil. Stir in paste, cream and combined stock and cornflour; bring to a boil. Simmer, uncovered, until slightly thickened.
Drain pasta and return to pan. Stir in sage, butter and spinach; stir until spinach is just wilted. Serve veal stroganoff over pasta mixture.

serves 4
per serving 26g fat; 2596kJ (621 cal)

spinach, capsicum and fetta pizzas

4 pitta bread (18cm round)
½ cup (125ml) tomato pasta sauce
2 cups (250g) grated pizza cheese
75g baby spinach leaves
1 medium red capsicum (200g), sliced thinly
100g fetta cheese, crumbled

Preheat oven to very hot.
Place pitta bread on oven trays, spread
with sauce.
Sprinkle half of the pizza cheese over pitta;
top with spinach, capsicum and fetta, sprinkle
with remaining pizza cheese.
Bake in very hot oven about 10 minutes
or until browned.

serves 4
per serving 21.6g fat; 2179kJ (521 cal)

spaghetti with zucchini, tomato and ricotta

500g spaghetti
1/4 cup (60ml) olive oil
4 medium zucchini (480g), cut into 5cm lengths
3 cloves garlic, sliced thinly
500g cherry tomatoes
100g baby rocket leaves
1 1/4 cups (250g) ricotta cheese

Cook pasta in large saucepan of boiling water until just tender; drain.
Meanwhile, heat oil in large frying pan, add zucchini; cook, stirring, until zucchini is just tender. Add garlic and tomatoes; cook, stirring occasionally, until tomatoes split and soften.
Combine hot pasta, tomato mixture and rocket in large bowl.
Serve spaghetti mixture topped with crumbled ricotta.

serves 4
per serving 23g fat; 2863kJ (685 cal)

veal cutlets with red pesto sauce

8 veal cutlets (900g)
1 tablespoon olive oil
200g button mushrooms, sliced
$1/2$ cup (125ml) beef stock
$1/3$ cup (80g) sun-dried tomato pesto
$1/2$ cup (125ml) cream
8 fresh basil leaves, torn

Cook veal on heated oiled grill plate (or grill
or barbecue) until browned on both sides
and cooked as desired.
Meanwhile, heat oil in medium frying pan;
add mushrooms, cook, stirring, until softened.
Add stock, pesto and cream; cook, stirring,
until hot, stir in basil.
Serve veal with red pesto sauce and, if desired,
steamed green beans and baby potatoes.

serves 4
per serving 28.6g fat; 1831kJ (437 cal)

salami and vegetable pasta

375g spiral pasta
2 tablespoons olive oil
1 large brown onion (300g), chopped
1 large red capsicum (350g), chopped
3 finger eggplants (180g), sliced thickly
150g sliced salami
400g jar tomato pasta sauce
2 tablespoons chopped fresh flat-leaf parsley
1/2 cup (40g) parmesan flakes

Cook pasta in large saucepan of boiling water,
uncovered, until just tender; drain.
Meanwhile, heat oil in large frying pan,
add onion, capsicum, eggplant and salami;
cook, stirring, until vegetables are tender.
Add sauce and parsley, stir until hot.
Combine pasta and vegetable mixture;
serve sprinkled with parmesan.

serves 4
per serving 28.5g fat; 2906kJ (694 cal)

lemon and olive lamb with couscous

1kg lamb backstrap (eye of loin)
1 cup (250ml) chicken stock
1 cup (200g) couscous
20g butter
2 tablespoons pine nuts
$\frac{1}{3}$ cup chopped fresh flat-leaf parsley
400g green beans
$\frac{1}{3}$ cup (80ml) dry white wine
$\frac{1}{2}$ cup (125ml) chicken stock, extra
1 tablespoon lemon juice
20g butter, chopped, extra
$\frac{1}{3}$ cup (50g) black olives

Cook lamb in large non-stick frying pan
until browned all over and cooked as desired.
Remove from pan, cover with foil; keep warm.
Meanwhile, bring stock to a boil in small saucepan.
Place couscous in medium heatproof bowl;
pour over hot stock. Stand about 5 minutes,
covered, or until liquid is absorbed.
Heat butter in small saucepan, add pine nuts;
cook, stirring, until browned lightly. Using a fork,
fluff couscous, then stir in pine nuts and parsley.
Boil, steam or microwave beans until just
tender; drain.
Drain excess fat from frying pan. Add wine to
pan, bring to a boil. Stir in extra stock and lemon
juice; simmer, uncovered, 1 minute or until reduced
slightly. Whisk in extra butter, then stir in olives.
Serve lamb and sauce with couscous and beans.

serves 4
per serving 22.6g fat; 2775kJ (664 cal)

chicken, basil and cabbage salad

You need to purchase a medium chinese cabbage for this recipe, as well as a large barbecue chicken weighing approximately 900g.

3 cups (480g) shredded cooked chicken
4 cups (320g) finely shredded chinese cabbage
4 green onions, sliced thinly
1/4 cup chopped fresh basil
1 teaspoon bottled crushed garlic
1/4 cup (60ml) peanut oil
1/4 cup (60ml) lime juice
2 tablespoons fish sauce
1 tablespoon sugar

Place chicken, cabbage, onion and basil in large bowl.
Combine garlic, oil, juice, sauce and sugar in screw-top jar; shake well.
Drizzle dressing over salad; toss gently to combine.

serves 4
per serving 19.9g fat; 1183kJ (283 cal)

steaks with green capsicum salsa

4 small beef eye fillet steaks (600g)
green capsicum salsa
2 small green capsicums (300g), chopped finely
1 small red onion (100g), chopped finely
1 medium red thai chilli, seeded, chopped
6 green onions, sliced
1/4 cup (60ml) lime juice
2 tablespoons chopped fresh mint

Cook beef on heated oiled grill plate (or grill
or barbecue) until browned on both sides
and cooked as desired.
Serve beef with green capsicum salsa and,
if desired, baby spinach leaves.
Green capsicum salsa Combine ingredients
in medium bowl.

serves 4
per serving 7.4g fat; 912kJ (218 cal)

creamy red pesto chicken with gnocchi

Fresh gnocchi is available refrigerated in supermarkets.

1 tablespoon olive oil
8 chicken thigh cutlets (1.3kg)
500g fresh gnocchi
1 teaspoon bottled crushed garlic
1/2 cup (125ml) dry white wine
1/4 cup (60g) sun-dried tomato pesto
300ml cream
1/4 cup loosely packed small fresh basil leaves

Heat oil in large frying pan, add chicken; cook, covered, until browned on both sides and cooked through.
Meanwhile, cook gnocchi in large saucepan of boiling water, uncovered, until tender; drain.
Remove chicken from pan, cover to keep warm. Drain fat from pan. Add garlic to pan; cook until fragrant. Add wine; simmer, uncovered, until most of the liquid has evaporated. Add pesto and cream; bring to a boil.
Serve chicken with gnocchi and sauce, sprinkled with basil.

serves 4
per serving 55.7g fat; 3668kJ (876 cal)

tandoori chicken salad

¹/₂ cup (140g) yogurt
1¹/₂ tablespoons tandoori paste
750g chicken tenderloins
³/₄ cup (200g) yogurt, extra
¹/₄ cup (60ml) mint sauce
250g mesclun
4 large egg tomatoes (360g), chopped
2 lebanese cucumbers (260g), chopped

Combine yogurt and paste in large bowl,
add chicken; stir until combined.
Cook chicken, in batches, on heated oiled
grill plate (or grill or barbecue) until browned
on both sides and cooked through.
Meanwhile, combine extra yogurt and
sauce in small bowl.
Divide mesclun among serving plates,
top with tomato, cucumber and chicken.
Serve drizzled with yogurt mint sauce.

serves 4
per serving 14.8g fat; 1545kJ (369 cal)

chicken sang choy bow

1 tablespoon peanut oil
1kg chicken mince
2 teaspoons bottled crushed garlic
230g can bamboo shoots, drained, chopped finely
1 teaspoon bottled chopped chilli
1 trimmed celery stick (75g), chopped finely
1 medium red capsicum (200g), chopped finely
2 tablespoons soy sauce
1 tablespoon rice vinegar
1½ tablespoons lime juice
2 teaspoons cornflour
½ cup (125ml) chicken stock
100g packet ready-to-serve fried noodles
¼ cup chopped fresh coriander
8 iceberg lettuce leaves, trimmed
soy sauce for serving, extra

Heat oil in large frying pan; cook chicken
and garlic over high heat, stirring, until chicken
changes colour.
Stir in bamboo shoots, chilli, celery, capsicum,
sauce, vinegar, juice and combined cornflour
and stock. Bring to a boil; simmer, uncovered,
until sauce thickens.
Just before serving, stir in noodles and coriander.
Serve chicken mixture in lettuce cups with
extra soy sauce, if desired.

serves 4
per serving 28.3g fat; 2113kJ (505 cal)

fast and fabulous desserts

Peel, core and thinly slice fresh pineapple; divide among serving plates. Drizzle with passionfruit pulp, Malibu and toasted flaked coconut.

Place a scoop of boysenberry ripple ice-cream into purchased meringue shells; serve drizzled with lemon curd.

Combine canned, drained peach slices with a little vanilla essence and ground cinnamon in individual serving dishes; top with coarsely crushed choc-chip cookies. Top with a little butter and brown sugar; cook in moderate oven until sugar melts and peaches are heated through.

Layer mascarpone, sliced bananas and crushed peanut brittle in a parfait glass.

Drizzle fresh ricotta with maple syrup; serve with mixed berries and toasted brioche.

Place canned, drained pear halves on pieces of ready-rolled puff pastry; roll in edges of pastry to meet pears. Sprinkle with brown sugar; bake in very hot oven until pastry is puffed and golden. Serve dusted with sifted icing sugar.

Top vanilla ice-cream with warm plunger coffee and Irish cream liqueur; serve with chocolate wafers.

Combine cream, chopped chocolate and marshmallows in saucepan; stir over low heat until melted and well combined. Serve chocolate fondue with fresh fruit.

glossary

bacon rashers also known as slices of bacon, made from cured and smoked pork.

bamboo shoots young, yellow shoots of bamboo plants; available fresh and in cans.

basil also known as sweet basil or common basil. Use leaves only; discard stems.

bean sprouts also known as bean shoots; new growths of germinated beans and seeds. Most readily available are: mung bean, soy bean, alfalfa and snow pea sprouts.

brioche a sweet, yeasty bread made with butter and eggs.

burghul also known as bulghur wheat; hulled, steamed wheat kernels that, once dried, are crushed into grains, in a variety of sizes.

butter use salted or unsalted (sweet) butter; 125g is equal to one stick of butter.

butter beans, canned cans labelled butter beans contain, in fact, cannellini beans. Large beige beans having a mealy texture and mild taste.

capsicum also known as bell pepper or, simply, pepper. They can be red, green, yellow, orange or purplish-black. Discard seeds and membranes before use.

celery salt blend of ground celery seed and salt; available in supermarkets.

cheese
fetta: white cheese with milky, fresh acidity; most commonly made from cow milk. Fetta is solid but crumbles readily.
mascarpone: fresh, unripened, smooth, triple-cream cheese with rich, sweet taste.

parmesan: also known as parmigiano, parmesan is a hard, grainy cow-milk cheese.
pizza: a commercial blend of processed grated mozzarella, cheddar and parmesan.
ricotta: a sweet, fairly moist, fresh curd cheese having a low fat content.

chilli
bottled chopped: conveniently chopped red chillies; available in jars from supermarkets.
sweet chilli sauce: mild, Thai-style sauce made from chillies, sugar, garlic and vinegar.
thai: range in colour from bright-red to dark-green, and taste medium-hot.

chinese broccoli also known as gai lum, gai larn and chinese kale.

chinese cabbage also known as peking or napa cabbage, wong bok and petsai; long cabbage with crinkly leaves.

ciabatta wood-fired Italian white bread with crisp crust.

coconut cream first pressing from grated coconut flesh; available in cans and cartons.

coconut milk second pressing (less rich) from grated coconut flesh; available in cans and cartons, also in lower-fat type.

coriander also known as cilantro or chinese parsley; leafy, green herb. Also sold in seed form, whole or ground.

cornflour also known as cornstarch; used as a thickening agent in cooking.

couscous fine, grain-like cereal product, made from semolina.

dijon mustard a pale brown, distinctively flavoured, fairly mild French mustard.

eggplant, finger also known as aubergine; small, finger-shaped eggplant.

essence also known as extract.

fennel seeds dried seeds having a licorice flavour.

fish sauce also called nam pla or nuoc nam; made from pulverised, salted, fermented fish. Has a pungent smell and strong taste; use sparingly.

fried noodles, ready-to-serve packaged crispy egg noodles, already deep-fried; also called crunchy noodles.

garlic, bottled conveniently crushed garlic; available in jars from supermarkets.

gnocchi dough shaped into balls, cooked in boiling water; generally made of potatoes.

green beans sometimes called french or string beans; this long fresh bean is consumed pod and all.

iceberg lettuce a heavy, firm round lettuce; has tightly furled leaves and crisp texture.

irish cream liqueur made from cream, irish whiskey and spirits; one brand is Baileys.

kaffir lime leaves aromatic leaves of a small citrus tree. Used fresh or dried, in a similar way to bay leaves.

kecap manis also called ketjap manis; an Indonesian sweet, thick soy sauce.

laksa paste commercial blend available from supermarkets.

lebanese cucumber also known as european or burpless cucumber.

leek a member of the onion family; resembles the green onion but is much larger.

lemon curd also known as lemon butter, lemon cheese or lemon spread.

lemon grass a lemon-smelling and -tasting grass; use only the white lower part of stem.

malibu brand-name of a rum-based coconut liqueur.

mango tropical fruit; fragrant deep-yellow flesh surrounds a large flat seed.

maple syrup distilled sap of the maple tree; available in supermarkets.

mayonnaise we used whole-egg mayonnaise.

mesclun a salad mix of assorted leaves.

mince also known as ground meat.

mint sauce available bottled in supermarkets.

naan bread leavened bread; traditionally baked against the inside wall of tandoor oven.

noodles

fresh egg: made from wheat flour and eggs; strands vary in thickness.

hokkien: fresh wheat-flour noodles resembling thick, yellow-brown spaghetti.

singapore: thin, dried egg noodles.

oil

olive: made from ripe olives. Extra virgin and virgin are the best, while extra light or light refers to taste not fat levels.

peanut: pressed from ground peanuts; has high smoke point.

sesame: made from roasted, crushed white sesame seeds.

onion

green: also known as scallion or (incorrectly) shallot; young onion picked before bulb has formed. Has long, green, edible stalk.

red: also known as spanish, red spanish or bermuda onion; sweet, large, purple-red onion.

oyster sauce sauce made from oysters and their brine, salt, soy sauce and starches.

paprika ground dried red capsicum (bell pepper); available sweet or hot.

parsley, flat-leaf also known as continental parsley or italian parsley.

passionfruit also known as granadilla; small tropical fruit with tough skin surrounding edible black, sweet-sour seeds.

peanut brittle a type of confectionery; choc-coated toffee and peanut bars.

pesto, sun-dried tomato commercial versions available in supermarkets.

pine nuts also known as pignoli; small, cream-coloured kernels.

pitta bread also known as lebanese bread. Wheat-flour pocket bread sold in large, flat pieces. Also available in small thick pieces as pocket pitta.

prawns also known as shrimp.

radicchio also known as red chicory; vegetable with reddish purple leaves and a mildly bitter flavour.

rocket also known as arugula, rugula and rucola; a peppery-tasting green leaf. Baby rocket leaves are less peppery.

soy sauce made from fermented soy beans. Available in supermarkets and Asian food stores.

spinach also known as english spinach and, incorrectly, silverbeet. Baby spinach leaves are also available.

stock available in cans or tetra packs. Stock cubes or powder can be used; 1 teaspoon stock powder or 1 small crumbled stock cube mixed with 1 cup water gives a strong stock.

sugar we used coarse, granulated table sugar, also known as crystal sugar, unless otherwise specified.

brown: an extremely soft, fine granulated sugar retaining molasses.

tandoori paste consists of garlic, tamarind, ginger, coriander, chilli and spices.

thai red curry paste consists of chilli, onion, garlic, oil, lemon rind, shrimp paste, cumin, paprika, turmeric and pepper.

tomato

cherry: also known as tiny tim or tom thumb tomatoes; small and round.

egg: also called plum or roma; smallish and oval-shaped.

paste: triple-concentrated tomato puree.

vinegar

balsamic: authentic only from Modena, Italy; made from white Trebbiano grapes aged in antique wooden casks.

red wine: based on fermented red wine.

rice wine: made from rice wine lees, salt and alcohol.

wasabi paste a hot, green, Asian horseradish paste.

wholegrain mustard also known as seeded; made from crushed mustard seeds and dijon-style mustard.

yogurt we used unflavoured, full-fat cow-milk yogurt unless stated otherwise.

zucchini also known as courgette.

index

facts & figures

These conversions are approximate only, but the difference between an exact and the approximate conversion of various liquid and dry measures is minimal and will not affect your cooking results.

Note: NZ, Canada, USA and UK all use 15ml tablespoons. Australian tablespoons measure 20ml. All cup and spoon measurements are level.

Measuring equipment

The difference between one country's measuring cups and another's is, at most, within a 2 or 3 teaspoon variance. (For the record, 1 Australian metric measuring cup holds approximately 250ml.) The most accurate way of measuring dry ingredients is to weigh them. For liquids, use a clear glass or plastic jug having metric markings.

How to measure

When using graduated measuring cups, shake dry ingredients loosely into the appropriate cup. Do not tap the cup on a bench or tightly pack the ingredients unless directed to do so. Level the top of measuring cups and measuring spoons with a knife. When measuring liquids, place a clear glass or plastic jug having metric markings on a flat surface to check accuracy at eye level.

Dry measures

metric	imperial
15g	1/2oz
30g	1oz
60g	2oz
90g	3oz
125g	4oz (¼lb)
155g	5oz
185g	6oz
220g	7oz
250g	8oz (½lb)
280g	9oz
315g	10oz
345g	11oz
375g	12oz (¾lb)
410g	13oz
440g	14oz
470g	15oz
500g	16oz (1lb)
750g	24oz (1½lb)
1kg	32oz (2lb)

We use large eggs having an average weight of 60g.

Liquid measures

metric	imperial
30 ml	1 fluid oz
60 ml	2 fluid oz
100 ml	3 fluid oz
125 ml	4 fluid oz
150 ml	5 fluid oz (¼ pint/1 gill)
190 ml	6 fluid oz
250 ml (1cup)	8 fluid oz
300 ml	10 fluid oz (½ pint)
500 ml	16 fluid oz
600 ml	20 fluid oz (1 pint)
1000 ml (1litre)	1¾ pints

Helpful measures

metric	imperial
3mm	⅛in
6mm	¼in
1cm	½in
2cm	¾in
2.5cm	1in
6cm	2½in
8cm	3in
20cm	8in
23cm	9in
25cm	10in
30cm	12in (1ft)

Oven temperatures

These oven temperatures are only a guide. Always check the manufacturer's manual.

	°C (Celsius)	°F (Fahrenheit)	Gas Mark
Very slow	120	250	1
Slow	150	300	2
Moderately slow	160	325	3
Moderate	180 –190	350 – 375	4
Moderately hot	200 – 210	400 – 425	5
Hot	220 – 230	450 – 475	6
Very hot	240 – 250	500 – 525	7

at your fingertips

These elegant slipcovers store up to 10 mini books and make the books instantly accessible.

And the metric measuring cups and spoons make following our recipes a piece of cake.

Book Holder
Australia and overseas:
$8.95 (incl. GST).

Metric Measuring Set
Australia: $6.50 (incl. GST).
New Zealand: $A8.00.
Elsewhere: $A9.95.
Prices include postage and handling. This offer is available in all countries.

Photocopy and complete coupon below

Mail or fax Photocopy and complete the coupon below and post to:
ACP Books Reader Offer, ACP Publishing, GPO Box 4967, Sydney NSW 2001, *or* fax to: (02) 9267 4967.

Phone Have your credit card details ready, then phone 136 116 (Mon-Fri, 8.00am-6.00pm; Sat, 8.00am-6.00pm).

Australian residents We accept the credit cards listed on the coupon, money orders and cheques.

Overseas residents We accept the credit cards listed on the coupon, drafts in $A drawn on an Australian bank, and also British, New Zealand and U.S. cheques in the currency of the country of issue. Credit card charges are at the exchange rate current at the time of payment.

Food director Pamela Clark
Food editor Louise Patniotis
ACP BOOKS STAFF
Editorial director Susan Tomnay
Creative director Hieu Chi Nguyen
Senior editor Julie Collard
Designer Mary Keep
Publishing manager (sales) Brian Cearnes
Publishing manager (rights & new projects) Jane Hazell
Brand manager Donna Gianniotis
Pre-press Harry Palmer
Production manager Carol Currie
Publisher Sue Wannan
Group publisher Pat Ingram
Chief executive officer John Alexander
Produced by ACP Books, Sydney.
Printing by Dai Nippon Printing in Korea.
Published by ACP Publishing Pty Limited, 54 Park St, Sydney; GPO Box 4088, Sydney, NSW 1028. Ph: (02) 9282 8618
Fax: (02) 9267 9438.
acpbooks@acp.com.au
www.acpbooks.com.au
To order books phone 136 116.
Send recipe enquiries to Recipeenquiries@acp.com.au
Australia Distributed by Network Services, GPO Box 4088, Sydney, NSW 1028.
Ph: (02) 9282 8777 Fax: (02) 9264 3278.
United Kingdom Distributed by Australian Consolidated Press (UK), Moulton Park Business Centre, Red House Road, Moulton Park, Northampton, NN3 6AQ. Ph: (01604) 497 531 Fax: (01604) 497 533 acpukltd@aol.com
Canada Distributed by Whitecap Books Ltd, 351 Lynn Ave, North Vancouver, BC, V7J 2C4, Ph: (604) 980 9852 Fax: (604) 980 8197
customerservice@whitecap.ca
www.whitecap.ca
New Zealand Distributed by Netlink Distribution Company, ACP Media Centre, Cnr Fanshawe and Beaumont Streets, Westhaven, Auckland. PO Box 47906, Ponsonby, Auckland, NZ.
Ph: (9) 366 9966 ask@ndcnz.co.nz

Clark, Pamela.
15-minute Feasts.

Includes index.
ISBN 1 86396 301 4

1. Quick and easy cookery.
I. Title. II. Title: 15-minute Feasts.
III. Title: Fifteen-minute Feasts.
IV. Title: Australian Women's Weekly.

641.555

© ACP Publishing Pty Limited 2003
Published 2003. Reprinted 2004.
ABN 18 053 273 546
This publication is copyright. No part of it may be reproduced or transmitted in any form without the written permission of the publishers.

Cover: Pork with white wine sauce, page 34.
Stylist: Kate Brown
Photographer: Chris Chen
Home economist for photography: Kelly Cruickshanks
Back cover: Left: Pork and chinese broccoli stir-fry, page 18; Right: Chicken, basil and cabbage salad, page 49.